FEB. 09

The Code of the Street and African-American Adolescent Violence

Findings and conclusions of the research reported here are those of the authors and do not necessarily reflect the official position or policies of the U.S. Department of Justice.

This research was supported by the National Institute of Justice (grant number 2005–IJ–CX–0035), the National Institute of Mental Health (MH48165, MH62669), and the Centers for Disease Control and Prevention (029136–02). Additional funding for this project was provided by the National Institute on Drug Abuse, the National Institute on Alcohol Abuse and Alcoholism, and the Iowa Agriculture and Home Economics Experiment Station (Project #3320).

NCJ 223509

ABOUT THIS REPORT

The "code of the street" theory, developed by Yale professor Elijah Anderson, presents an explanation for high rates of violence among African-American adolescents. Observing life in a Philadelphia African-American neighborhood, Anderson saw that economic disadvantage, separation from mainstream society, and racial discrimination encountered by some African-American adolescents may lead to anti-social attitudes and to violent behavior.

This Research in Brief presents research exploring Anderson's thesis; researchers conducted repeated interviews with more than 800 African-American adolescents (ages 10 to 15) and their primary caregivers in Georgia and Iowa over a two-year period. The researchers looked for developmental relationships between neighborhood and family characteristics, reported experiences with racial discrimination, expressed street code values and self-reported violent behavior in young people.

What did the researchers find?

The results generally support Anderson's original observations: the stress of living in a poor and violent environment can cause young people to adopt the code of the street as a lifestyle guide. This, in turn, is a powerful predictor of violent conduct, amplified by the effects of negative neighborhood characteristics.

Why is this research important?

Anderson's theory presents a bridge between the environmental and cultural factors examined in many previous studies of urban violence. The research discussed in this report emphasizes the need to consider this theory in future studies within African-American households, neighborhoods and communities.

Eric A. Stewart and Ronald L. Simons

The Code of the Street and African-American Adolescent Violence

For several decades, researchers have studied the race/violence relationship. A number of explanations have been put forth to clarify the forces at play behind this relationship.[1] Elijah Anderson, a professor of sociology currently at Yale University,[2] presents a compelling argument for the high rates of violence among African-American adolescents. In his "code of the street" thesis,[3] Anderson argues that the economic disadvantage, social dislocation and racial discrimination encountered by some African-American adolescents foster deviant, anti-social attitudes (i.e., a street code) and developmental pathways that are related to violent behavior. (See "Synopsis of the Street Code.")

This Research in Brief looks at the results of research into the validity of the "code of the street" theory. The authors reviewed two waves of surveys with more than 800 African-American adolescents (ages 10 to 15) and their primary caregivers

About the Authors

Eric A. Stewart is an Associate Professor in the College of Criminology and Criminal Justice at Florida State University, a member of the National Consortium on Violence Research and a National Institute of Justice W.E.B. DuBois Fellow. Ronald L. Simons is a Distinguished Research Professor of Sociology and a Research Fellow with the Institute for Behavioral Research at the University of Georgia.

SYNOPSIS OF THE STREET CODE

by Elijah Anderson

Of all the problems besetting the poor, inner-city black community, none is more pressing than that of interpersonal violence and aggression. It wreaks havoc daily with the lives of community residents and increasingly spills over into downtown and residential middle-class areas. Muggings, burglaries, carjackings and drug-related shootings, all of which may leave their victims or innocent bystanders dead, are now common enough to concern all urban and many suburban residents. The inclination to violence springs from the circumstances of life among the ghetto poor — the lack of jobs that pay a living wage, the stigma of race, the fallout from rampant drug use and drug trafficking, and the resulting alienation and lack of hope for the future.

Continued on page 2

Continued from page 1

Simply living in such an environment places young people at special risk of falling victim to aggressive behavior. Although there are often forces in the community that can counteract the negative influences — by far the most powerful being a strong, loving, "decent" (as inner-city residents put it) family committed to middle-class values — the despair is pervasive enough to have spawned an oppositional culture, that of "the streets," whose norms are often consciously opposed to those of mainstream society. These two orientations — decent and street — socially organize the community, and their coexistence has important consequences for residents, particularly children growing up in the inner city. Above all, this environment means that even youngsters whose home lives reflect mainstream values — and the majority of homes in the community do — must be able to handle themselves in a street-oriented environment.

This is because the street culture has evolved what may be called a code of the street, which amounts to a set of informal rules governing interpersonal public behavior, including violence. The rules prescribe both a proper comportment and the proper way to respond if challenged. They regulate the use of violence and so supply a rationale that allows those who are inclined to aggression to precipitate violent encounters in an approved way. The rules have been established and are enforced mainly by the street oriented, but on the streets the distinction between street and decent is often irrelevant; everybody knows that if the rules are violated, there are penalties. Knowledge of the code is thus largely defensive; it is literally necessary for operating in public. Therefore, even though families with a decency orientation are usually opposed to the values of the code, they often reluctantly encourage their children's familiarity with it to enable them to negotiate the inner-city environment.

At the heart of the code is the issue of respect — loosely defined as being treated "right" or granted the deference, or "props," one deserves. However, in the troublesome public environment of the inner city, as people increasingly feel buffeted by forces beyond their control, what one deserves in the way of respect becomes more and more problematic and uncertain. This in turn further opens the issue of respect, or "street credibility," to sometimes intense interpersonal negotiation. In the street culture, especially among young people, "street cred" is viewed as almost an external entity that is hard-won but easily lost, and so must constantly be guarded; it is high maintenance, and is never secured once and for all but depends on a series of performances that effectively answer challenges and transgressions by others.

It is in this way that one's street credibility is established, and when possessed and successfully claimed, it works to deter advances; with the right amount, a person can avoid "being bothered" in public. In fact, the rules of the code provide a framework for negotiating street credibility. The person whose very appearance — including his clothing, demeanor and way of moving — deters transgressions can feel that he possesses, and may be considered by others to possess, a measure of respect; he is reminded of this by the way he is treated and regarded. Hence, if he is bothered and advances against his person are made, not only may he be in physical danger, but he has been disgraced or "dissed" (disrespected) and often feels vulnerable to further, and possibly more serious, advances.

Though many of the forms that dissing can take might seem petty to middle-class people (maintaining eye contact for too long, for example), on the streets, being dissed is always consequential. Particularly to those invested in the street code, such actions become serious indications of the other person's intentions; left unanswered, they can seriously erode one's street credibility. Consequently, young people become very sensitive to advances and slights, which could well serve as a warning of imminent physical confrontation or danger.

This hard reality can be traced to the profound sense of alienation from mainstream society and its institutions felt by many poor, inner-city black people, particularly the young. The code of the streets is actually a cultural adaptation to a profound lack of faith in the police and the judicial system. The police are most often seen as representing the dominant white society and not caring to protect inner-city residents. When called, they may not respond, which is one reason many residents feel they must be prepared to take extraordinary measures to defend themselves and their loved ones against those who are inclined to aggression. Lack of police accountability has in fact been incorporated into the local status system: the person who is believed capable of "taking care of himself" is accorded a certain deference, which translates into a sense of physical and psychological control. Thus the street code emerges where the influence of the police and the justice system ends and personal responsibility for one's safety is felt to begin. When respect for the civil law erodes, "street justice" fills the void, thus underscoring the need for street credibility to operate on the streets of the local community. Exacerbated by the proliferation of drugs and easy access to guns, this volatile situation promises those with unassailable street credibility, often the street-oriented minority, the opportunity to dominate the public spaces.

in Georgia and Iowa (see "Sampling Methodology"). The survey asked about delinquent behavior, experience with racial discrimination, and certain attitudes associated with the code of the street. The authors also looked at geographic, family and economic factors in the environments of these young people. They examined whether neighborhood and family characteristics, racial discrimination and adoption of street code values predict later violent behavior.

The study discussed here reinforces a line of research stressing the importance of looking at the developmental living conditions and experiences that shape urban culture and contribute to violence.[4] Among the study's findings:

- Anderson's theory is generally supported by this study.

- The data suggest that neighborhood characteristics (specifically, a climate of violence and economic disadvantage) increase violent behavior.

- Young people who had experienced racial discrimination were more likely to engage in violent behavior.

- Living in a family that is "decent" — a family that shares mainstream American values — appears to lower the risk of violent conduct.

- Living in the opposite of a decent family — a "street" family — does not appear to raise the risk of violent conduct in the first and second waves of the study. This may indicate that street families appear to encourage their children to represent street values only on the surface (as a protective mechanism) and not in practice.

- Most significantly, the study showed that a youth's expressed street code attitude is a developmental predictor of violent behavior two years later. It seems that those who internalized the code and actually lived by it were more likely to be involved in later reported acts of violence.

These findings are discussed in greater detail in the "Conclusions" section (p. 14).

Sampling Methodology

Characteristics of the Sample

This study is based on the first two waves of data from the Family and Community Health Study (FACHS), a multisite investigation in Georgia and Iowa of neighborhood and family effects on an individual's health and development. FACHS was conducted by the Center for Family Research at the University of Georgia. The first wave, which was collected in 1997, consisted of 867 African-American adolescents (400 boys and 467 girls; 462 in Iowa and 405 in Georgia) ages 10 to 13 years old and their primary caregivers. In the second wave, which was collected in 1999, 738 of the adolescents (now ages 12 to 15) and their caregivers were again surveyed. This represents a retention rate of 85 percent from 1997 to 1999. Analyses indicated that the families who did not participate in wave 2 did not differ significantly from those who participated with regard to caregiver income and education or target child's age, gender, school performance or delinquency. Complete data for the variables used in this study were available for 720 families.

In Georgia, families were recruited from portions of the Atlanta metropolitan area, such as South Atlanta, East Atlanta, Southeast Atlanta and Athens. In Iowa, all study participants resided in two metropolitan urban communities: Waterloo and Des Moines.

Sampling Strategy

The sampling strategy for FACHS was designed to meet the study's goal of investigating the effects of neighborhood characteristics on the functioning of children and families. The families were recruited from neighborhoods that varied as to demographic characteristics (i.e., percent African-American) and economic level (i.e., percent of families with children living below the poverty line). The final sample of families recruited involved participants who ranged from extremely poor to middle class. The sampling strategy yielded a relatively representative set of communities with sufficient variability in economic status to allow detection of significant relations between community characteristics and outcome variables.

In both Georgia and Iowa, families were drawn randomly from rosters and contacted to determine their interest in participation. Of the families on the rosters who could be located, interviews were completed with 72 percent of eligible Iowa families and just over 60 percent of eligible Georgia families.

Compensation

Respondents were reimbursed for participating in the study. Primary caregivers received $100 and target children received $70. The reimbursement levels reflected the different amounts of time required of each family member for participation.

Characteristics related to adoption of the street code

Neighborhood characteristics. Anderson argues that the high rates of poverty, joblessness, violence, racial discrimination, alienation, mistrust of police and hopelessness that typify many disadvantaged neighborhoods have instilled anti-social attitudes and values in some residents. Although most families who reside in disadvantaged neighborhoods are law abiding, everyone in the neighborhood learns or knows the rules of the street code to be followed and possible penalties for violating these rules. Adolescents are likely to be taught violent behavior, to witness violent acts and to have role models who display high levels of aggression and violence. As a result, these youngsters present a bravado or a sense of pride in being tough, present a violent identity and protect themselves and their close friends with threats of violence or with actual violent behavior. Living in such circumstances places adolescents at increased risk for falling victim to violence. As more people adopt defensive behaviors, the level of violence tends to escalate and the number of people who rely on violence increases.[5]

Decent and street families. Another aspect of the code of the street thesis distinguishes between "decent" and "street" families[6] living in disadvantaged African-American neighborhoods.

As Anderson notes, most families in disadvantaged African-American neighborhoods are decent people. Decent families value hard work and self-reliance, and encourage their children to avoid trouble. These families tend to accept mainstream values and try to instill these values in their children. Because of the dangers found in disadvantaged environments, decent families tend to be authoritative and watchful in their parenting styles and are cognizant of unfavorable peers and problem behaviors that may be presented by their own children.

On the other hand, Anderson indicates that street families have lives that are disorganized and filled with anger, hostility, physical altercations and other anti-social behaviors. Street families may frequently engage in ineffective parenting strategies, such as yelling, poor supervision, verbal insults, and the harsh and inconsistent discipline entrenched in the code of the street. Anderson suggests that street families may socialize their children accordingly. They may encourage their children to follow the street code and adopt the attitude that violence can be used to gain or maintain respect. For these parents, the code of the street may provide meaning and pride in their lives, as their social identities are entwined with the street culture.

Racial discrimination.

Anderson also discusses the harmful effects of racial discrimination and its role in fostering the street code. He suggests that experience with racial discrimination fosters

perceptions of injustice, helplessness and despair among African-American adolescents. Those who experience discrimination come to perceive the system, and those who represent it, as unfair. They believe that they cannot rely on authorities to prevent reoccurrences. These perceptions may serve to justify the adolescents' violation of mainstream beliefs and values. They come to believe that they must take matters into their own hands to protect themselves, leading to use of street code behaviors as a means of self-defense. In addition, victims of discrimination may perceive few options for addressing their situations because reporting such events may make them be seen as weak and invite further victimization. The risk associated with such outcomes may lead adolescents to protect themselves by adopting unconventional beliefs and by exhibiting antisocial behaviors.

Testing the code of the street thesis

To test the code of the street theory, interviews with adolescents and their caregivers were examined. Various factors, including the adoption of street

Exhibit 1. Study Controls

The control variables used in this study included family socioeconomic status (SES); family structure; number of children per household; target child's gender, association with violent peers, school attachment and experience with stress; and neighborhood type and location.

Family SES	Measured by primary caregiver education level and family income. These two items were standardized and summed to form a composite measure of family SES.
Family structure	A dichotomous variable denoting households in which there were two caregivers in the home in comparison with single-caregiver homes (1=two-caregiver family, 0=one-caregiver family).
Number of children per household	Set as the aggregate number of children under the age of responsibility residing in the home of the primary caregiver more than half of the time.
Target gender	A dichotomous variable, with 1=male and 0=female (the reference group).
Association with violent peers	Measured by three items adapted from the National Youth Survey Family Study (NYSFS),[a] which asked respondents how many of their close friends had engaged in violent acts. The responses to the items were summed to obtain a total score regarding the extent to which the respondents' friends engaged in violent behavior.[b]
School attachment	Measured by a 12-item scale that indicated the extent to which the respondents cared about school and had positive feelings toward school. The items were summed to create an index of school attachment.[c]
Strain (stress level)	Measured by the summed total of affirmative responses to 15 events that may cause strain or emotional discomfort, such as breaking up with a boyfriend or girlfriend or failing a class.[d]
Urban	A dichotomous variable indicating neighborhoods located in a city (=1) with nonurban neighborhoods (=0) as the reference group.
South	A dichotomous variable indicating neighborhoods located in the southern United States, i.e., Georgia (=1) with Midwestern, i.e., Iowa, neighborhoods (=0) as the reference group.

[a] NYSFS follows a group of individuals originally surveyed in 1976 when they were between the ages of 11 and 17 years old to look at their changing attitudes, beliefs and behaviors about topics such as career goals, involvement with community and family, violence, drugs and social values. See Elliott, D.S., D. Huizinga, and S. Menard, *Multiple Problem Youth: Delinquency, Substance Use, and Mental Health Problems,* New York: Springer-Verlag, 1989. For other publications on the NYSFS, see http://www.colorado.edu/ibs/NYSFS/currentresearchers/menardpublications.html.

[b] The alpha coefficient for the scale was .68.

[c] The alpha coefficient was .79.

[d] The KR_{20} coefficient was .77.

code values, were analyzed to see if they predict later violent behavior. The authors controlled for a variety of factors that have been shown to affect violent behaviors (see exhibit 1).

Measuring neighborhood characteristics. Two indexes were constructed to represent neighborhood characteristics: neighborhood violence and neighborhood disadvantage. Neighborhood violence measured the extent to which violent acts (e.g., fights, gang violence, drug violence, robbery, homicide and aggravated assaults) were reported to be a problem within the neighborhood. The neighborhood disadvantage index was formed using five census variables as markers of economic disadvantage: proportion of households headed by women, proportion of persons on public assistance, proportion of households below the poverty level, proportion of persons unemployed and proportion of African-Americans.[7]

Measuring family characteristics. To identify family characteristics, a behavioral rating system based on observations was used to assess the quality of behavioral exchanges and interactions between family members. Ratings of family interactions relied on the ability of trained observers to judge overall characteristics of the individuals and groups being observed.[8] Fourteen different rating scales were used to identify family characteristics.[9] The "decent" family category was measured using seven of the observed behaviors (consistent discipline, child monitoring, positive reinforcement, quality time, warmth and support, inductive reasoning and pro-social behavior).[10] The "street" family category was measured using the remaining seven observed behaviors (inconsistent and harsh discipline, hostility, physical attacks, parental violence, verbal abuse, anti-social behavior and child neglect).[11]

Measuring racial discrimination. Racial discrimination was measured using the adolescents' responses to 13 items from the Schedule of Racist Events, a list of experiences with racial discrimination developed in the 1990s.[12] These items assessed how often the adolescents reported perceived experiences with various discriminatory events over the past year. Questions included:

- How often has someone yelled a racial slur or racial insult at you just because you are African-American?

- How often have the police hassled you just because you are African-American?

- How often has someone threatened you physically just because you are African-American?

Other items focused on disrespectful treatment by sales clerks, false accusations by authority figures and exclusion from social activities because of being African- American.[13]

Measuring adoption of the street code. Adoption of the street code was measured with a seven-item, self-report scale on which adolescents were asked to indicate the extent to which they thought it was justifiable or advantageous to use violence in certain situations (1=strongly disagree to 4=strongly agree). Statements included:

- When someone disrespects you, it is important that you use physical force or aggression to teach him or her not to disrespect you.

- If someone uses violence against you, it is important that you use violence against him or her to get even.

- People will take advantage of you if you don't let them know how tough you are.

- People do not respect a person who is afraid to fight physically for his or her rights.

- Sometimes you need to threaten people in order to get them to treat you fairly.

- It is important to show others that you cannot be intimidated.

- People tend to respect a person who is tough and aggressive.[14]

Measuring violent behavior. Self-reported violent behavior was measured using eight questions to assess violent offending. Respondents answered a series of questions regarding how often during the preceding year they had engaged in various violent acts (e.g., physical assault, threatening others, bullying others, using a weapon and robbing others). Nearly 28 percent of the sample reported engaging in violent behavior during the last year.

Exhibit 2. **Descriptive Statistics and Correlations for the Study Variables**

	Mean	S.D.	Self-Reported Violent Behavior$_{T2}$
Controls			
Family SES	12.57	4.14	-.05
Family Structure (1=two parents)	.52	.50	-.03
Target Gender (1=male)	.46	.50	.16[a]
Number of Children	2.67	1.32	.06
Violent Peers	4.21	1.72	.23[a]
School Attachment	27.39	5.48	-.15[a]
Strain	6.23	2.67	.04
Urban	.52	.48	.05
South	.49	.46	.08[b]
Self-Reported Prior Violent Behavior$_{T1}$	1.46	1.91	.45[a]
Family Characteristics			
Decent Family	19.87	3.47	-.15[a]
Street Family	16.12	5.48	.03
Discrimination			
Racial Discrimination	21.76	6.64	.12[a]
Neighborhood Characteristics			
Neighborhood Violence	11.56	4.37	.12[a]
Neighborhood Disadvantage	-.03	1.00	.09[b]
Dependent Variables			
Street Code$_{T2}$	17.22	3.61	.25[a]
Self-Reported Violent Behavior$_{T2}$	2.18	3.29	——

[a] $p < .01$, [b] $p < .05$

N=720

Relating adoption of the street code to violent behavior

Descriptive statistics and bivariate correlations for all variables included in this study are presented in exhibit 2. The results show that neighborhood violence, neighborhood disadvantage, experience with racial discrimination and adoption of the street code are significantly related to later reported violent behavior. Furthermore, belonging to "decent" families has a significant and negative association with self-reported violence; but surprisingly, belonging to "street" families does not at all appear to be related to violent behavior reported two years later.

Measures with significant relationships to violent behavior. Analyses were performed to examine the effects of neighborhood context, family characteristics, racial discrimination and street code adoption on later violent behavior. The results in exhibit 3 indicate that being male, associating with violent peers, having a history of violent involvement, experiencing discrimination, living in a neighborhood characterized by violence and disadvantage, and adopting

the street code are significant predictors of later reported violent behavior. Conversely, being attached to school and living in a decent family are significant predictors of not engaging in violent behavior.

Exhibit 4 graphically presents the results of an advanced logistical regression analysis with six variables. Of the variables examined, adopting the street code had the strongest effect on violence. This is consistent with Anderson's assertion that the code of the street is highly related to elevated levels of violence.[15] Indeed, only prior violent behavior had a stronger predictive effect from the first to second interviews two years later (see exhibit 2).

Further, a reciprocal effects model, used to estimate the directional relationship between violent behavior and the code of the street (see exhibit 5), indicated that while the standardized path coefficient from violent behavior$_{T2}$ to street code$_{T2}$ (.10) is significant, the coefficient from street code to violent behavior (.25) is significant to a higher degree. Additional analysis (using the equality of coefficient test)[16] confirmed that the path from street code to violent behavior is

Exhibit 3. Regression Coefficients of Self-Reported Violent Behavior$_{T2}$ on Control, Family, Discrimination, Neighborhood and Street Code Variables

	Model 1		
	Coef.	**S.D.**	**z-value**
Independent Variables			
Controls			
Family SES	.013	.081	.160
Family Structure (1=two parents)	-.063	.052	-1.211
Target Gender (1=male)	.237	.053	4.472[a]
Number of Children	-.017	.019	-.895
Violent Peers	.189	.056	3.375[a]
School Attachment	-.191	.055	-3.537[a]
Strain	.021	.034	.618
Urban	.024	.028	.857
South	.042	.041	1.024
Self-Reported Prior Violent Behavior$_{T1}$	.467	.036	12.972[a]
Family Characteristics			
Decent Family	-.160	.053	-3.019[a]
Street Family	-.034	.059	-.576
Discrimination			
Racial Discrimination	.102	.053	1.925[b]
Neighborhood Characteristics			
Neighborhood Violence	.101	.052	1.942[b]
Neighborhood Disadvantage	.092	.053	1.736[b]
Code of the Street			
Street Code$_{T2}$	.246	.052	4.731[a]
Overdispersion parameter	-.545	.141	-3.865[a]
Model X^2 (df)	198.17(16)		
Pseudo R^2	.259		

[a]$p = < .01$, [b]$p = < .10$

$N=720$

Standardized coefficient weights are presented.

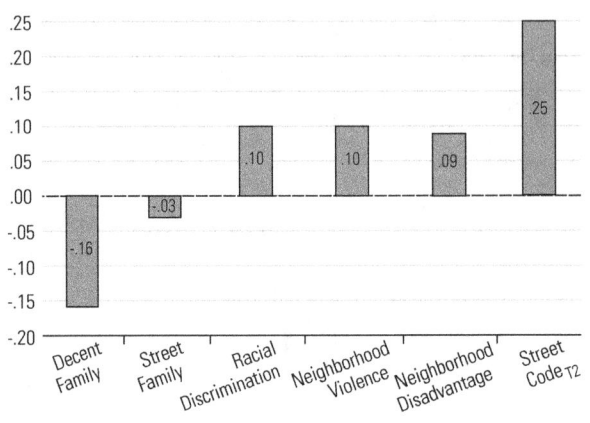

Exhibit 4. Negative Binomial Regression Coefficients of Self-Reported Violent Behavior$_{T2}$ on Family, Discrimination, Neighborhood and Street Code Variables

significantly different from and stronger than the path from violent behavior to street code. This finding lends support to the notion that adopting the street code leads to delinquent behavior rather than delinquent behavior leading to the adoption of the street code.

Conclusions. Drawing on insights from Anderson's code of the street thesis, this study examined whether neighborhood problems, family characteristics, racial discrimination and street code values explain violent behavior. The results were generally consistent with Anderson's

thesis. They suggest that family characteristics, racial discrimination, neighborhood context and street code values are significant predictors of violence.

In particular, being raised in a "decent" family appears to lower the risk of being involved in violence. This suggests that decent families serve an important socializing function in reducing violent behavior and victimization.

An unexpected finding was that the "street" family variable was not related to self-reported violent behavior two years later. This may

Exhibit 5. Model Showing the Reciprocal Relationship Between Street Code and Self-Reported Violent Behavior

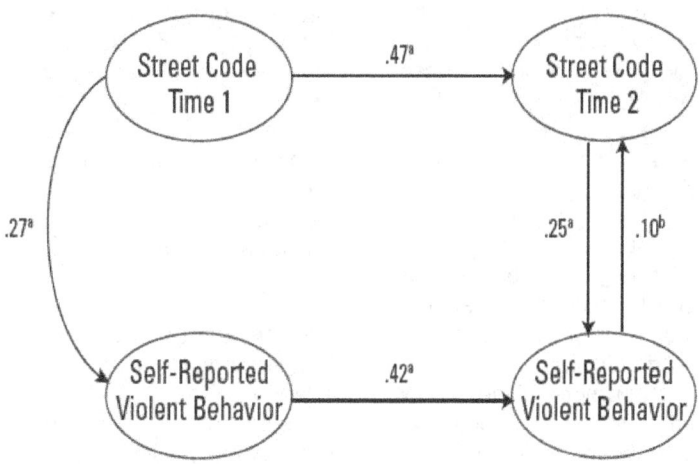

Notes: $N = 720$, $X^2 = 2.61$, $p = .151$, GFI = .99, AGFI = .98, RMSEA = .042
Coefficients are standardized.
Measurement error correlation is controlled.
The Squared Multiple Correlation was .27 for Street Code$_{T2}$ and .23 for Self-Reported
   Violent Behavior$_{T2}$
[a]$p < .01$, [b]$p < .05$

suggest that although street families may encourage their children to adopt and present the street code, they do not directly influence them to engage in later violence. Thus, it is possible that street families use the threat of violence, the "code," as a form of deterrence. Although street families embrace the street code, they may use violence only when necessary. If this is the case, reliance on street justice may deter would-be perpetrators from

attacking because of fear of retribution and escalating levels of violence, and might actually serve to prevent some violence.[17]

A third finding was that reported experience with racial discrimination significantly predicted self-reported violent behavior. Experiencing discrimination may lead to a perception that society is unfair, and victims of discrimination may come to believe that aggression and violence are legitimate mechanisms for solving grievances. This finding suggests that conceptual frameworks and comprehensive explanations for violence among African-Americans may be incomplete if they do not account for experience with racial discrimination.

The results also suggest that neighborhood structural conditions may influence violent behavior. Specifically, neighborhood violence and neighborhood disadvantage are significant predictors of adolescent violence. Several other studies have observed that a disproportionate number of individuals living in disadvantaged and dangerous neighborhoods see their chances of gaining conventional success and respect as limited.[18] Therefore, disadvantaged, high-crime neighborhoods may generate alternative routes to gaining respect, such as adopting the code of the street and engaging in violent lifestyles.[19]

Last, and most important, the study showed that an individual adolescent's adoption of the street code (as opposed to simply being part of a street code family) is a powerful antecedent of violence. The results point to

an amplifying effect, where neighborhood problems foster violence and adopting the street code further increases the risk of violence. This result adds to the growing literature that describes how neighborhood characteristics combine with deviant cultural codes to perpetuate violence in communities (in this case, African-American communities).[20]

Researchers interested in studying the race/violence relationship should appreciate elements of Anderson's code of the street thesis. Anderson's thesis bridges the environmental-cultural divide inherent in many urban violence studies. It is hoped that the findings in this study will encourage better understanding and increased interest in how neighborhood conditions, family characteristics, racial discrimination and street code values work together to inflame violent behavior.

Notes

1. See, e.g., Elliott, D.S., "Serious Violent Offenders: Onset, Developmental Course, and Termination — The American Society of Criminology 1993 Presidential Address," *Criminology*, 32 (1) (February 1994): 1–21; Farrington, D.P., "Predictors, Causes, and Correlates

of Male Youth Violence," in *Crime and Justice: A Review of Research,* vol. 24, ed. Michael Tonry and Mark H. Moore, Chicago: University of Chicago Press, 1998: 421–475; Hawkins, D.F., J.H. Laub, J.L. Lauritsen, and L. Cothern, *Race, Ethnicity, and Serious and Violent Juvenile Offending,* Juvenile Justice Bulletin, Washington, DC: U.S. Department of Justice, Office of Juvenile Justice and Delinquency Prevention, June 2000, NCJ 181202; Moore, M.H., and M. Tonry, "Youth Violence in America," in *Crime and Justice: A Review of Research,* vol. 24, ed. Michael Tonry and Mark H. Moore, Chicago: University of Chicago Press, 1998: 1–26; Office of Juvenile Justice and Delinquency Prevention, *Report to Congress on Juvenile Violence Research,* Washington, DC: U.S. Department of Justice, Office of Juvenile Justice and Delinquency Prevention, 1999, NCJ 176976; Reiss, A.J., and J.A. Roth, *Understanding and Preventing Violence,* Washington, DC: National Academy Press, 1993.

2. At the time he developed his theory discussed here, Professor Anderson was affiliated with the University of Pennsylvania.

3. Anderson, E., "The Code of the Streets," *Atlantic Monthly* 273 (5) (May 1994): 80–94; Anderson, E., *Code of the Street: Decency, Violence, and the Moral Life of the Inner City,* New York: W.W. Norton and Company, 1999.

4. Anderson, *Code of the Street* (see note 3). See also Bruce, M.A., V.J. Roscigno, and P.L. McCall, "Structure, Context, and Agency in the Reproduction of Black-on-Black Violence," *Theoretical Criminology* 2 (1998): 29–55; Kubrin, C.E., and R. Weitzer, "Retaliatory Homicide: Concentrated Disadvantage and Neighborhood Culture," *Social Problems,* 50 (2) (May 2003): 157–180; Sampson, R.J., and W.J. Wilson, "Toward a Theory of Race, Crime, and Urban Inequality," in *Crime and Inequality,* ed. John Hagan and Ruth D. Peterson, Stanford, CA: Stanford University Press, 1995: 37–54.

5. Anderson, *Code of the Street* (see note 3). See also Baumer, E., J. Horney, R.B. Felson, and J.L. Lauritsen, "Neighborhood Disadvantage and the Nature of Violence," *Criminology* 41 (1) (February 2003): 39–72; Oliver, W., *The Violent Social World of Black Men,* New York: Lexington Books, 1994.

6. Anderson used the terms "decent" and "street" to characterize the families that he studied. The authors of this Research in Brief are in no way imposing a moral judgment by suggesting that "decent" families are good and "street" families are bad.

7. Factor analysis indicated that these variables loaded on a single factor for the block group areas (BGAs) in the sample. The items were standardized and combined to form a measure of disadvantage. The alpha coefficient was .89.

8. Melby, J., R.D. Conger, R. Book, M. Rueter, L. Lucy, D. Repinski, S. Rogers, B. Rogers, and L. Scaramella, *Iowa Family Interaction Rating Scales,* Ames, IA: Iowa Youth and Families Project, 1998.

9. The statistical program AMOS (Arbuckle, J. L., and W. Wothke,

AMOS Users' Guide Version 4.0, Chicago: Smallwaters Corporation, 1999) was used to create single-factor, latent variables for the decent and street family constructs. Each of the observed indicators of the latent variable was specified as a linear combination of a latent factor plus random measurement error. In each case, assessment of the overall measurement models demonstrated that the items selected to measure the theoretical constructs "decent" and "street" were statistically significant.

10. Maximum likelihood estimation analysis indicated that the items loaded on a common construct and ranged from .55 to .88. The correlations between the items ranged from .48 to .89. The alpha coefficient was .81.

11. Maximum likelihood estimation analysis indicated that the items loaded on a common construct and ranged from .53 to .89. The correlations between the items ranged from .47 to .91. The alpha coefficient was .84. The correlation between decent and street families is -.49.

12. Landrine, H., and E.A. Klonoff, "The Schedule of Racist Events: A Measure of Racial Discrimination and a Study of Its Negative Physical and Mental Health Consequences," *Journal of Black Psychology* 22 (2) (1996): 144–168.

13. The alpha coefficient for the scale was .85.

14. The alpha coefficient for this measure was .78 for the first set of interviews and .80 for the second set of interviews. It is clear that this measure of Anderson's code of the street may not capture all of the complexities he identified. Most important to the research discussed here are the attitudinal components of the code of the street.

15. Anderson, *Code of the Street* (see note 3).

16. Paternoster, R., R. Brame, P. Mazerolle, and A. Piquero, "Using the Correct Statistical Test for the Equality of Regression Coefficients," *Criminology* 36 (4) (November 1998): 859–866.

17. This conclusion is supported by Kubrin and Weitzer, "Retaliatory Homicide: Concentrated Disadvantage and Neighborhood Culture" (see note 4).

18. Bruce et al., "Structure, Context, and Agency in the Reproduction of Black-on-Black Violence" (see note 4); Kubrin and Weitzer, "Retaliatory Homicide: Concentrated Disadvantage and Neighborhood Culture" (see note 4).

19. Anderson, *Code of the Street* (see note 3); Bruce et al., "Structure, Context, and Agency in the Reproduction of Black-on-Black Violence" (see note 4); Oliver, *The Violent Social World of Black Men* (see note 5).

20. Bruce et al., "Structure, Context, and Agency in the Reproduction of Black-on-Black Violence" (see note 4); Kubrin and Weitzer, "Retaliatory Homicide: Concentrated Disadvantage and Neighborhood Culture" (see note 4); Sampson and Wilson, "Toward a Theory of Race, Crime, and Urban Inequality (see note 4).

Additional reading

Baron, S.W., L.W. Kennedy, and D.R. Forde. "Male Street Youths' Conflict: The Role of Background, Subcultural, and Situational Factors." *Justice Quarterly* 18 (2001): 759–789.

Baumrind, D. "The Influence of Parenting Style on Adolescent Competence and Substance Use." *Journal of Early Adolescence* 11 (1991): 56–95.

Bellair, P.E. "Social Interaction and Community Crime: Examining the Importance of Neighbor Networks." *Criminology* 35 (1997): 677–701.

Bellair, P.E., V.J. Roscigno, and T.L. McNulty. "Linking Local Labor Market Opportunity to Violent Adolescent Delinquency." *Journal of Research in Crime and Delinquency* 40 (2003): 6–33.

Berkowitz, L. "Frustration-Aggression Hypothesis: Examination and Reformulation." *Psychological Bulletin* 106 (1989): 59–73.

Bernard, T.J. "Angry Aggression Among the Truly Disadvantaged." *Criminology* 28 (1990): 73–96.

Cao, L., A. Adams, and V.J. Jensen. "A Test of the Black Subculture of Violence Thesis: A Research Note." *Criminology* 35 (1997): 367–379.

Cloward, R., and L. Ohlin. *Delinquency and Opportunity.* Glencoe, IL: Free Press, 1960.

Cohen, A.K. *Delinquent Boys.* Glencoe, IL: Free Press, 1955.

Courtwright, D.T. *Violent Land: Single Men and Social Disorder from the Frontier to the Inner City.* Cambridge, MA: Harvard University Press, 1996.

DuBois, W.E.B. *The Philadelphia Negro: A Social Study.* Philadelphia: University of Pennsylvania Press, 1899 (reprinted 1996).

Fagan, J., and D.L. Wilkinson. "Firearms and Youth Violence." In *Handbook of Antisocial Behavior,* ed. David Stoff, James Brieling, and Jack D. Maser. New York: John Wiley and Sons, 1997.

Furstenberg, F.F., T.D. Cook, J. Eccles, G.H. Elder, Jr., and A. Sameroff. *Managing to Make It: Urban Families and Adolescent Success.* Chicago: University of Chicago Press, 1999.

Hawkins, D.F. "Editor's Introduction." In *Violent Crime: Assessing Race and Ethnic Differences,* ed. Darnell F. Hawkins. New York: Cambridge University Press, 2003.

Hawkins, D.F., J.H. Laub, J.L. Lauritsen, and L. Cothern. *Race, Ethnicity, and Serious and Violent Juvenile Offending,* Juvenile Justice Bulletin. Washington, DC: U.S. Department of Justice, Office of Juvenile Justice and Delinquency Prevention, 2000.

Jarrett, R.L. "African-American Children, Families, and Neighborhoods: Qualitative Contributions to Understanding Developmental Pathways." *Qualitative Sociology* 20 (1997): 275–288.

Luckenbill, D.F., and D.P. Doyle. "Structural Position and Violence: Developing a Cultural Explanation." *Criminology* 27 (1989): 801–818.

Markowitz, F.E., and R.B. Felson. "Social-Demographic Attitudes and Violence." *Criminology* 36 (1998): 117–138.

McCord, J., and M.E. Ensminger. "Racial Discrimination and Violence: A Longitudinal Perspective." In *Violent Crime: Assessing Race and Ethnic Differences,* ed. Darnell F. Hawkins. New York: Cambridge University Press, 2003.

Miller, W.B. "Lower Class Culture as a Generating Milieu of Gang Delinquency." *Journal of Social Issues* 14 (1958): 5–19.

Simons, R.L., Y.-F. Chen, E.A. Stewart, and G.H. Brody. "Incidents of Discrimination and Risk for Delinquency: A Longitudinal Test of Strain Theory With an African-American Sample." *Justice Quarterly* 20 (2003): 827–854.

Sullivan, M.I. *Getting Paid: Youth Crime and Work in the Inner City.* New York: Cornell University Press, 1989.

Tedeschi, J., and R.B. Felson. *Violence, Aggression, and Coercive Action.* Washington, DC: American Psychological Association Books, 1994.

Wilkinson, D.L. *Guns, Violence, and Identity Among African-American and Latino Youth.* New York: LFB Scholarly Publishing, 2003.

Wolfgang, M.E., and F. Ferracuti. *The Subculture of Violence: Towards an Integrated Theory of Criminology.* London: Tavistock, 1967.

The National Institute of Justice is the research, development, and evaluation agency of the U.S. Department of Justice. NIJ's mission is to advance scientific research, development, and evaluation to enhance the administration of justice and public safety.

The National Institute of Justice is a component of the Office of Justice Programs, which also includes the Bureau of Justice Assistance; the Bureau of Justice Statistics; the Community Capacity Development Office; the Office for Victims of Crime; the Office of Juvenile Justice and Delinquency Prevention; and the Office of Sex Offender Sentencing, Monitoring, Apprehending, Registering, and Tracking (SMART).